GLASS DOLL

J. JOYCE LEA

Copyright © 2023
J. Joyce Lea
Glass Doll
All rights reserved.

No part of this publication may be reproduced, distributed, or transmitted in any form or by any means, including photocopying, recording, or other electronic or mechanical methods, without the prior written permission of the publisher, except in the case of brief quotations embodied in critical reviews and certain other non-commercial uses permitted by copyright law.

J. Joyce Lea

Printed Worldwide
First Printing 2023
First Edition 2023

10 9 8 7 6 5 4 3 2 1

Acknowledgments

This project focuses on fragility, vulnerability, and the hurt that comes along with love and loss. Pain is often paired with growing older and learning how to be comfortable being on your own, and finding balance between loving deeply and caring for yourself can be challenging on top of learning how to be an adult. I worked on this project during one of the most emotionally turbulent periods of my life, and have since emerged from it being a lot stronger. I'd like to thank my mother for being the first poet I ever knew, and I give my thanks to my best friends, Lexie and Kris, who mean the world to me. Much love.

Table of Contents

Movement 1
Scrape 3
City 5
Lasso 7
Patient 9
Veil 11
End 13
Arms 15
Wall 17
Strength 19
Age 21
Venus 23
Neck 25
Morning 27
Hair 29
Dagger 31
Mother 33
Jester 35
Rooftop 37
Car 39
Stitches 41
Ghost 43
Feminine 45
Levee 47
Towel 49
Smile 51
Reflection 53
She 55
Haunted 57

Body	59
Corrode	61
Grin	63
Door	65
Fade	67
Fragile	69
Mail	71
July	73
Longing	75
Ragdoll	77
Illness	79
Storm	81
Contort	83
Specimen	85
Eternal	87
Martyr	89
Silence	91
365	93
Surrender	95
Downfall	97
Apparition	99
Alone	101
Growing	103
Grave	105
War	107
Dreams	109
Someday	111

Movement

think of me
when the rose oil spills
and the blood
lies dormant on white sheets
where we once laid
eternalized in linen
sweet wind
hisses with the broken radiator
think of me
when you hear
the trains
and know impulse
keeps me moving
never far
i'm never free
from you
and the balcony.

- j.

SCRAPE

no need for
bandages
as your body leaves
the scene
without a scrape
wrapping and wrapping
i keep
pouring
through the cloth.

- j.

CITY

cigarette in hand
i scream at the skyline
the city laughs
at my bruised ego
cutting, chasing
another paycheck
blown in brooklyn
the day subsides
nighttime cascades
over restless streets,
my weary eyes weep
as i scream out
"where is my dream?"

- j.

Lasso

a love
my arms
weren't long enough
to grasp.
grabbing a lasso,
hurling the rope
as it bloodies my palms
into the sky
screaming
sobbing
longing
for someone,
anyone.
i reel the rope
back
and the sky
oh,
how she laughs.

- j.

Patient

fill me with elixir
in the deathbed you crafted
medicate me
until air is fresh
in battered lungs
count the trees
in an outside world
seen behind glass
poison my flowing blood
so i may never
watch them grow.

- j.

Veil

adorn myself in a veil
for whomever.
i fear i'll never be a bride.
white was never
my color.
but i set the table
with two wine glasses
weeping, lipstick all over.
make me beautiful
for a night
or two.

   -   j.

End

i knew the end
when the sight of your face
did not falter my breath,
widen my eyes.
the rosy scent
i gave you
is mine again
in a bottle
in my dresser.
planes
will always fly
to you
without me
seated
dreaming out
of their windows.

   -   j.

ARMS

asleep
in my arms
aching more than i used to
a second skin that no longer fits,
give the shirt off your back
for me to fold.

tell me stories
you've never told another
lashes flutter
hearts wrinkle and writhe
sweet flinches and jolts
lost in a dreamscape.

my body is riddled with illness
and left with patches
where brown hair once sprouted
you
are just as beautiful
as i remembered.

how i've longed for
your perfect pains,

that singe and sear
and now i know
that when my arms are empty once more,
you were never mine to hold.

- j.

WALL

between my soul
and a heart willing to mend it
brick by brick
unwavering and cold,
chapped lips and false hopes
i release and inflict

shielded, standing
i cannot be
battered, bruised

without sound
without tears
unbeknownst to you
i place another brick.

- j.

STRENGTH

come with hurt,
bring me your worst
come with fire, come with rain
so i may weather any storm
you bring
plastered with
a broken smile
and pretending
that i'm strong enough
to endure it all.

- j.

AGE

an old soul
plagued with
a new world.
staring and watching
wading through passing streetlights
sitting in crowded cars
music blares,
laughter and smiles
this is not my home,
home is not my home
"what's on your mind, doll?"
it won't matter
when morning comes.

- j.

Venus

heavenly mother
watches every step
i take
when a lover calls
my name.

venus, i was made
from the blood
spilt from wars
that fought for your love
venus, i forever reach
for your gentle hand.

venus, i have loved
venus, i have lied
venus, i will do it
again and again.

- j.

NECK

the tightness in my throat
holding onto longing
when i never know
what to long for
words
that never escape my lips
months of quiet
subside
as i lay helpless
with my flesh surrounding your fingers.

flushed cheeks and
a hand around my neck
while i pray
you never release
your grasp
around it
and never release the words
stored within it.

- j.

Morning

show me the ones
you've loved and lost
sing of them
until my ears ache
come with ten, twenty
wrapped around your charm
in the daylight.

come to me
and leave them
at the front door
when the light of morning
returns to blind
your eyes.

- j.

Hair

running my fingers
through what remains
of me
i look like a dream
my shower drain
disagrees
thinned and frail,
though the praise
never ceases.
always adored
as i fall apart.

- j.

DAGGER

unsheath yourself
through flesh
all warmth
surrounds you
my insides pour
out
as they always do
at the steel gates.

- j.

Mother

mother taught me
how to roll my clothes
mother taught me
how to fit in a suitcase
mother taught me
that one glass
is never enough
mother held me
when the pills
didn't fix me
i'm sorry i'm sorry i'm sorry
mother i'm hurting
i'm writing
mother, they'll never love me
i'm dancing
i'm sobbing alone
mother i'm
just like you.

- j.

JESTER

twirling
around
with eyes,
glimmer, gawking
the lace, the jewels,
am i charming
am i lovely
the necklace bruises my throat
laughing
as i spin
crying
when the curtain
closes.
you all
adore
the fool
that dances.

- j.

Rooftop

my family loves me,
my cat does too.
burnt fingertips, running
out of time
moving, speeding, torturous time.
it will never
spare me.
peering over
the edge,
my legs hang
it would be so easy
but
my family loves me
and my cat does too.

- j.

CAR

you leave again
in a car
on the street.
you leave me with
a gift not meant for me,
a false hope
of reconnection
i'll hold tightly.

stay a little longer,
watch me corrode
in the daylight,
listen to
my breathing
in the night
and drive off
when morning comes again.

- j.

Stitches

tell me
of all that you lack.
eyes
that see only flesh.
i tear off grafts
of my skin
to stitch you
back together.
take the tools
i used
to fix you
before you're
far away.
hear my wails
echo in the sky
as you go.

- j.

Ghost

fingers interlocked
we exist
under blankets
and christmas lights.
gentle apparition
dances with me.
ghostly lover
holds my tears
in their hands
so they may
never fall.
and i awake
with sheets too clean.

- j.

FEMININE

french pressed coffee
gentle nudges from my cat
rose oil
dancing alone
cleaning up
pink candle wax

pain in my abdomen
unanswered letters
unreciprocated love
fake house plants
tears on
silk pillowcases

i have
my mother's nose
and her mother's
signature
on my wrist.

- j.

LEVEE

ever since
the levee broke,
there have been
talks over breakfast
the mornings after
i do everything
i told myself
not to.

how foolish it is
giving gifts
to lovers who
wouldn't dare
place flowers
on my stone.

- j.

TOWEL

look in my eyes
steal what is mine
yours, you, all yours
take me
want me
marry me for
fifteen minutes
and
leave me out
to dry.
don't bother
cleaning me
when you're finished.
leave me without
a goodnight
and fall asleep
in another room.

- j.

Smile

far, far from you
as your hand
rests on my thigh
in a crowded room.
a drink, maybe two
maybe three
maybe until
i smile
and you love
my smile.
maybe four
maybe until
i'm teary-eyed
alone on the bathroom floor
wishing you'd help me back up
and you hate
my tears.

- j.

Reflection

scars,
eye bags,
consequences
of impulsivity.
cheekbones more hollow
than they were.
pale, tired doll
looks at me,
teary-eyed
in the mirror.

it's just
you and i
isn't it.

- j.

SHE

when i lay my head
to rest,
she tells me
the goodnights
i always
long to listen to.

she waits for
my eyes to open
every morning.
making my bed
after gently lifting me
up
to start my day.

she makes sure
i finish my meals.
she says i'm
so pretty.
she plays me
my favorite songs.

i make

crying messes
that she cleans up
"you know
i always
love you so."

when teary eyes
catch a glimpse,
she looks lovely
in the bedroom mirror.

- j.

Haunted

sleep in a bed
that was
never mine
never meant
for me.

live the
lonely little life
i lost
everything for.

when noise
wouldn't cease,
no one
heard my cries.

a soul left
unsatisfied
will forever haunt
the four white walls
you call your own.

- j.

Body

oh, face
your beauty
captivates
when you try
hard enough.

oh, hands
you couldn't have
held on
any tighter
to the ones
that ran away.

oh, body
you've been
loved, bruised, left
alone again
alone in your bed
alone with the
lights on.

- j.

CORRODE

you watched
months of
her corrosion
as
she loved
loved
loved you so much
loved you until
bronze turned a pale green
and she
couldn't love
any longer.

- j.

GRIN

is it me
that you want
or is it the way
i bat my lashes
at your words

are those words
for me
or are they for
her

the one i see
in performances
perfectly scripted
perfectly tied together

the one that
enters my mirror
every now and then
and looks back at me
muttering through a toothy grin

"you won't be
this beautiful
forever."

- j.

DOOR

you made your way in
so forcefully
splintering your fist
through my locked door
to hold
my hand.

- j.

FADE

i'll let you go
where i know
you won't return

i'll let you fade
into a blur

and when i see
that old blur
every once in a while

i'll smile,
knowing that crying
won't bring you back.

    -   j.

FRAGILE

you're only pretty
when you're begging
me
to care about you.

i assigned myself
a role
i cannot
play,
can't you see that
i don't have the time to
entertain you?

i don't want you
finding comfort
when you hear
my heartbeat's rhythm
in the night
because it beats
for someone
else.

you're made of glass

and you're only pretty
when you're begging
me
to love you.

brainless, thoughtless doll,
can't you see
that i
never will?

- j.

Mail

i mailed you
letters
that sat upon
your nightstand
as you slept in
other beds.

wrapped my
body
in satin
tied with ribbons.
every scar of yours
was a scar of
mine
and all i wanted
was to
charm my way
through the
distance.

wishing you'd
mail yourself back
into my arms

i sat
waiting,
but my mailbox
collected dust
as those autumn nights
went
on
and
on.

    -   j.

July

drunk under
a full moon
on too much
cherry flavored vodka
at a bar
i never took you to
with friends
you never met
and with a nauseated head
resting on a car window
i say
"i am free now".

- j.

LONGING

passing through
the streets i know
on the way home
and i only seem
to see the beauty
of this little city
when i'm drinking
when i'm longing to
go back to bed
when i can't afford
to be anywhere
else.

- j.

Ragdoll

when i see
a pretty limb
or eyelash
or piece of cloth
on another,
i pluck and pull it
off
and attach it
to myself.

constructed
of all the parts
i admire
in others,
i am stitched together
with pretty pink
thread
who am i
but a poorly constructed
ragdoll

who am i
but pieces
who am i.

- j.

ILLNESS

a diseased body
an ill mind
seeking comfort beneath
the same blanket
when the day is done.
i work the same job
i drink the same coffee
i carry the same illness
with me
i cure myself for a moment
only to get worse
i get worse and worse
i fear
this is all
i'll ever know.
i'll just be
worse.

- j.

STORM

i am
the eye of
the storm
that dismantled
the home
you built
for yourself.
i am the wind
that shredded
your skin.
i am the water
that filled
your lungs.
i had plenty of time
to build up my momentum
and
i wasn't finished
until you and i were
nothing and nowhere.

- j.

CONTORT

if i cannot be
your only
i would like to be
your favorite.
though i cannot contort
my form
into anyone you'd like,
i will try
and try
until my limbs ache
and my skin bruises
and i rest my head
on your lap
and you tell me
how good i am
for trying.

- j.

Specimen

i watch him
as he watches others.
i study his every move
memorize every gesture
each and every interest
so i can mold myself into
a form he'd like to
keep looking at.

oh, how i long to be
the specimen he studies,
getting excitement out of
each new discovery he makes.

but i'm not under any microscope
i'm not laid out on any tray
i am my face.
i am my body.
amongst all the other faces
and bodies
he sees.
to him,
there is nothing to be studied.

to him,
i am nothing more
than my form.

- j.

ETERNAL

my old friend,
i remember the cursive tattoo you had
right below your collarbone
i remember how you
drove us around
when we both felt like dying
i remember the cigarettes
out the window
and onto the west hill streets.
i'll remember you always
and how you said
we'd be eternal.

- j.

Martyr

oh, dear martyr
it's never your fault.
oh, dear martyr
your whining falls
on deaf ears.
oh, martyr you
endured such hardship
didn't you
oh, dear martyr
i'm so glad
i'm nothing
like you.

- j.

Silence

my closure
is your silence
and i must live with that
forever
as i cannot bear
to hear
your voice
that once spoke the words
"i'm not going anywhere"
list all the reasons why
you couldn't stay.

- j.

365

three hundred and sixty five
days
have passed me by
and though
the cut has healed,
i was left with
a scar
that i'll douse with
rose oil
and kiss goodnight
every night
for another
three hundred and sixty five
more.

- j.

Surrender

and there i stood
waving a white flag
plastered with a tired smile
and a body riddled
with an illness
that knows no cure.

please don't
hurt me anymore
i don't have any fight left in me
i'm tired i'm tired i'm so tired
can't you see
but i am slashed open
again
so everyone can see
if i'd bleed more
than last time.

   - j.

DOWNFALL

you're nostalgic for chaos
and you know
you're not in love
falling, trembling
those caresses in
the night
mean nothing
to you
nothing at all
because you yearn for a disaster
that will never come again
and pray for a downfall
you'll never see.

- j.

Apparition

an untouched cup of coffee
will forever sit
on the bedside table
and it waits and waits
and i will forever be
on the other end
of the line
when the medicine
doesn't work.

if i ever fall asleep again,
please visit me
as i dream
and please don't appear
as yourself.
appear as light
shining through the apartment windows
in the morning.
appear as warm wind
rustling through palm leaves
in the night.
come to me as
a fabricated form

i'll only hold
if my hands do not
pass through it
as they would through
cigarette smoke
on the drive home.

i wait and wait
for an apparition
to find me on the balcony
but i always wake up
before it gets the chance
to speak.

- j

Alone

you and i were
a household name
in my dream last night
and my heart still asks me
to pick up a phone
that never rings.
my body lives
in the city
where i am everything
and nothing and
i'm so so happy
carrying groceries on the train home
and writing and crying and listening
i'm so alone
and i'm not lonely in the slightest.

- j.

Growing

no matter how many new beds
i sleep in
or how many new cats i live with,
there will always be
a part of me
in the passenger seat of
childhood friends cars
in our little suburbia
talking about how things once were.
i wish i spent more time
with all of them
and got them more gifts
on all of their birthdays.
i wish i never once closed my door
when my mom wanted to
spend time with
her only daughter.
i wish i never took
a single moment for granted.
i've grown so much
yet never tall enough to outgrow my little bed
and there are times where
i wish i could stay

in my little life
in my little bed
forever
and tell my mom i love her
at her doorway
each night.

- j.

GRAVE

smooth the dirt over
bit by bit
with a shovel,
you are part of earth
more than before
you lie as you did in life
i cannot crawl in
the hollows you found yourself
asleep and pale
and burrow with you
sit with your cold flesh
as we rot and rot
into her core
together, always
but sometimes
i must stop myself
from trying.

- j.

War

war is just a byproduct of my love
and every letter i wrote
mapped out the catalyst of destruction
i brought to this world.
all i wanted was love
but gnawing on bones and
avenging each slash made across my skin
with much deeper cuts
into the skin of their makers
scarring so they will never forget,

that is how my gentle heart
must pass the time now
to become even gentler.

- j.

DREAMS

and i have dreamed so much of you
for better or for worse
and in these dreams
i rest all sorrows
in the palm of your hand
as you hold them
kindly.

here you are,
dancing in my mind
a rosary swaying
in front of
drunken starry eyes
like a pendulum
hypnotizing me
in a world where you smile
with your teeth.

cleansed of your crimes
and returned to your living form
only until my eyes meet

the morning sunlight
again
and again.

and i have dreamed
so much of you.

    -   j.

Someday

the tears
don't escape.
love ungiven
finds its home.
lost, little doll
sleeps soundly
beside
a beating heart
that loves her so,
whomever that may be.

the fan is whirring,
there is no plane
no train
to strip away
this dream
in this liminal early morning.

here,
she finally
sleeps.

- j.

Made in the USA
Columbia, SC
14 February 2025